#GodsLoveJournal

📷 @NewHopeRBC + @NotYoGrandMaMasBibleStudy
📘 @NewHopeRBC + @NotYoGrandMaMasBibleStudy
🖱️ NewHopeRBC.com

Copyright © 2025 by D Nicole Williams

All rights reserved.

No portion of this publication may be reproduced, distributed, or transmitted in any form or by any means, including photocopying, recording, or other electronic or mechanical methods, without the prior written permission of the publisher, except in the case of brief quotations embodied in critical reviews and certain other noncommercial uses permitted by copyright law.

For permission requests, email the publisher, addressed "ATTN: Permissions" at the following: NewHope@NewHopeRBC.com

Bulk discounts are available on quantity purchases by associations, corporations, and others for business, educational and ministry use. For details, contact the publisher at the address above.

ISBN: 978-1-942650-41-6

Pastor,
I wish for you...

In the Mighty Name of Jesus.
Amen

"THE LORD IS MY LIGHT AND MY SALVATION—WHOM SHALL I FEAR?"
Psalm 27:1

weekly GRATITUDE

Name one thing you're grateful for daily.

I tell you the truth, you can say to this mountain,
'May you be lifted up and thrown into the sea,'
and it will happen.   Mark 11:23

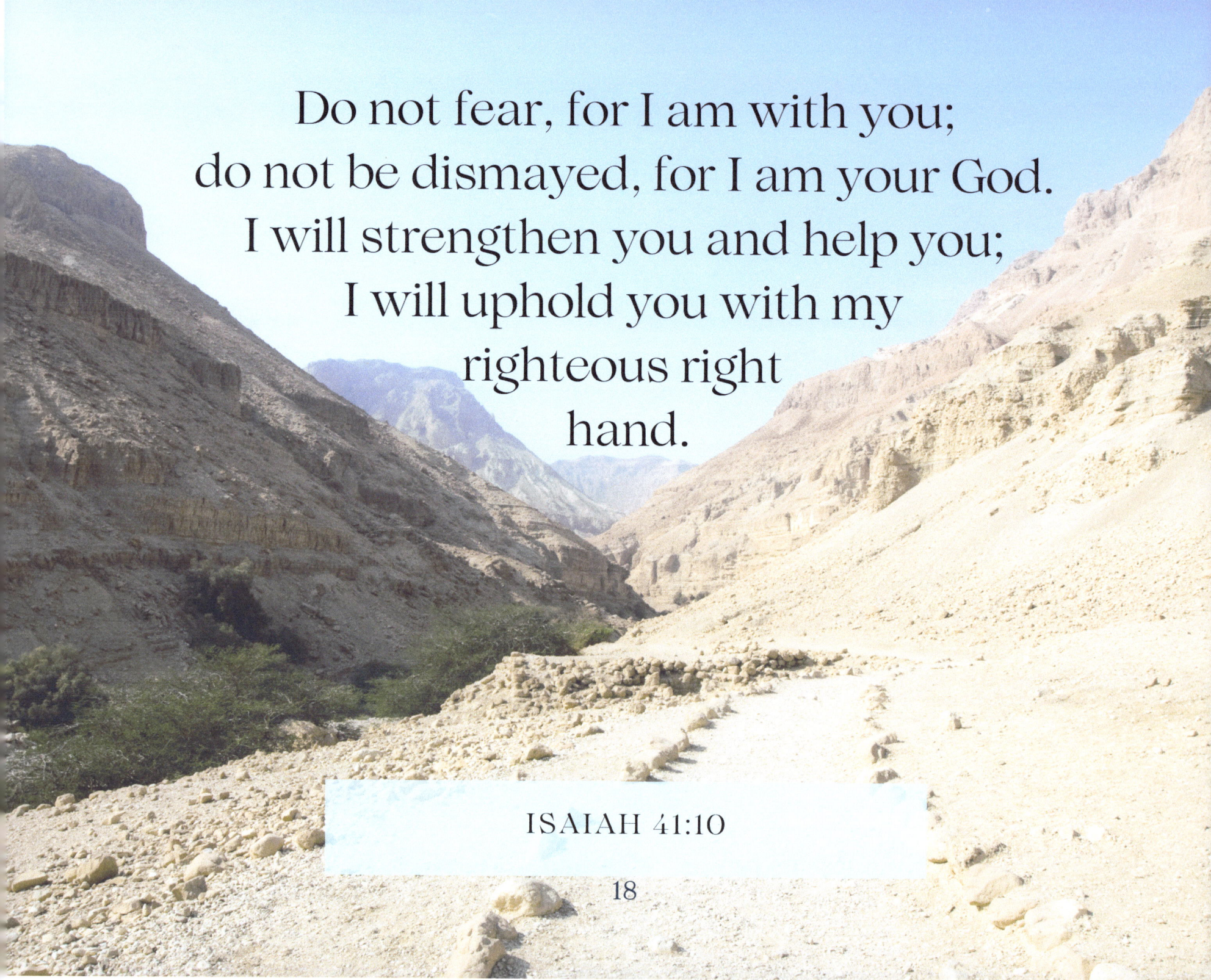

Do not fear, for I am with you;
do not be dismayed, for I am your God.
I will strengthen you and help you;
I will uphold you with my
righteous right
hand.

ISAIAH 41:10

19

"When I am afraid,
I put my trust in You."

Psalm 56:3

3 Ways to Trust God More Today

1. **PRAY FIRST**
2. **GIVE THANKS DAILY**
3. **LET GO OF FEAR**

3

1.
2.
3.

3

1.
2.
3.

3

1.
2.
3.

What's your go-to WORSHIP SONG?

REMINDER

REMINDER

God's timing is perfect.
Keep trusting Him!

LIES	TRUTH
"I am not enough."	"I will never leave you nor forsake you." (Hebrews 13:5)
"God doesn't care about me."	"For I know the plans I have for you, declares the Lord." (Jeremiah 29:11)

LIES	TRUTH
"I am alone."	"You are fearfully and wonderfully made." (Psalm 139:14)
"I have no purpose."	"Cast all your anxiety on Him because He cares for you." (1 Peter 5:7)

WHAT DOES ROMANS 8:28 REALLY MEAN?

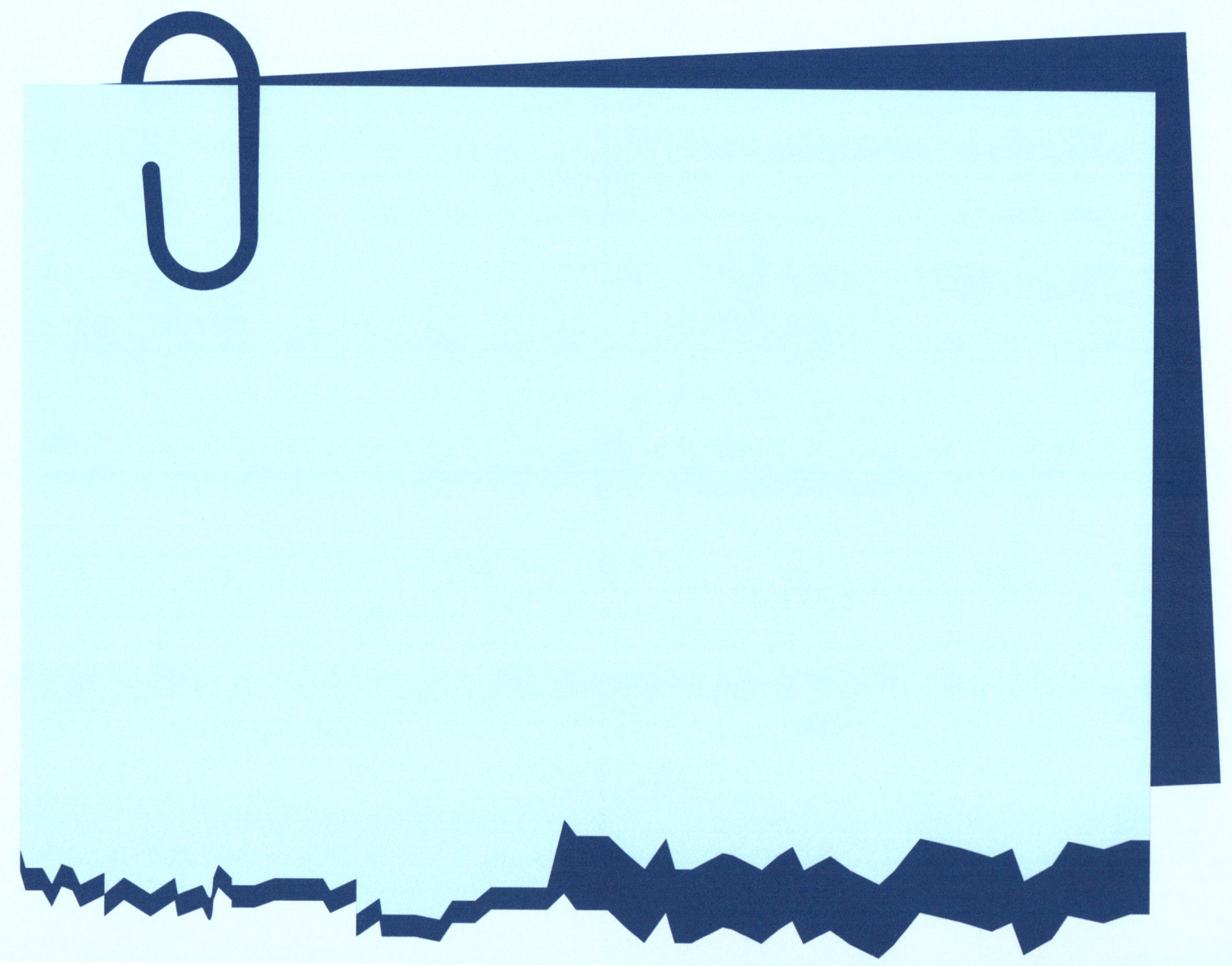

"It reminds us that God works ALL things for our good, even when we don't see it."

"HE WILL COVER YOU WITH HIS FEATHERS, AND UNDER HIS WINGS YOU WILL FIND REFUGE."

Psalm 91:4

GOD'S PROMISES FOR YOU:

I will never leave you — *Hebrews 13:5*

I am your strength — *Isaiah 41:10*

I have plans to prosper you — *Jeremiah 29:11*

"BE STILL, AND KNOW THAT I AM GOD."

Psalm 46:10

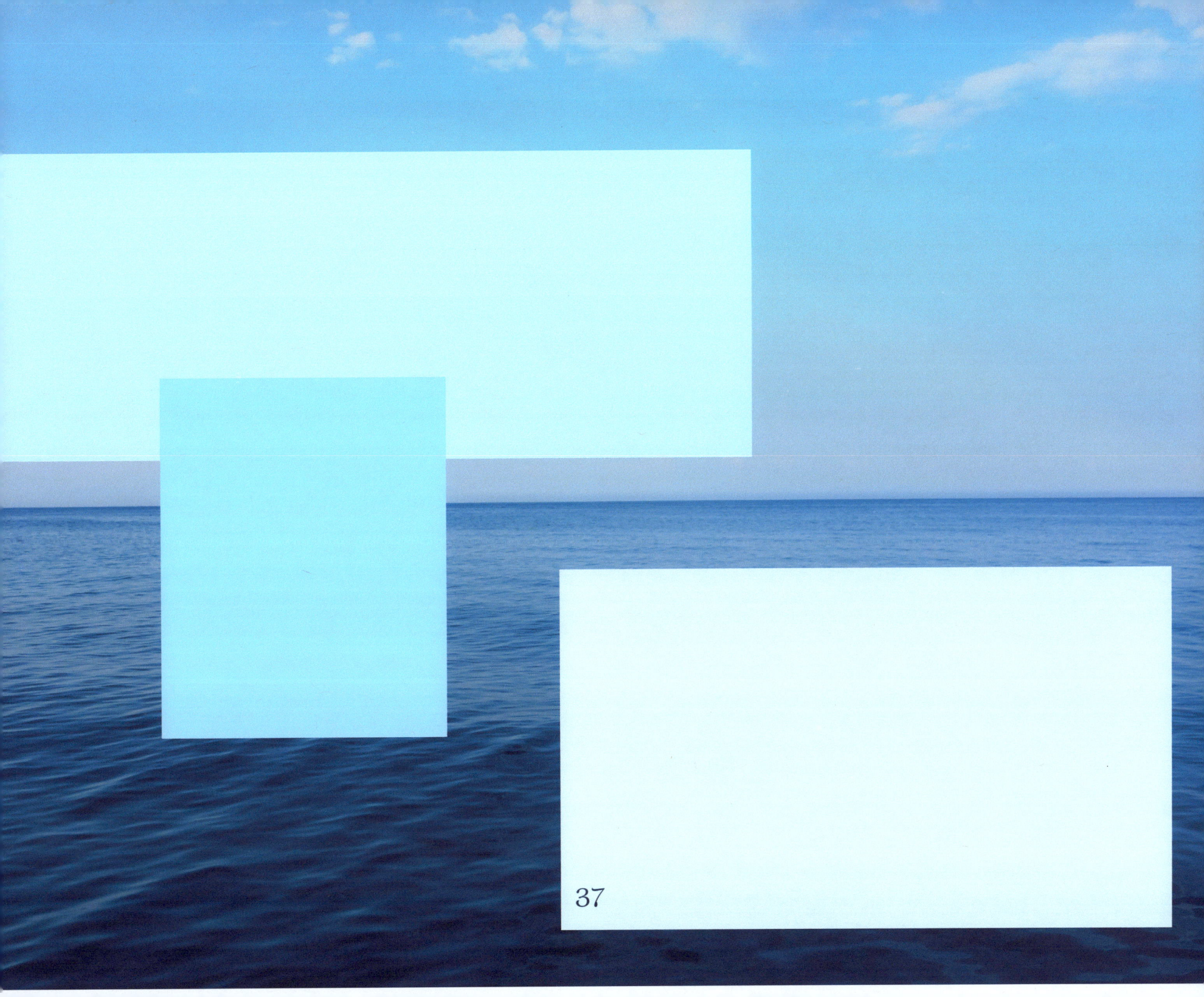

"All Scripture is God-breathed and is useful for teaching, rebuking, correcting and training in righteousness, so that the servant of God may be thoroughly equipped for every good work."

2 Timothy 3:16-17

Psalm 46:1

"God is our refuge and strength,
an ever-present help in trouble."

Many blessings from God!

495 PSALMS 26–28

Teach me your way, LORD;
    lead me in a straight path
    because of my oppressors.
Do not turn me over to the desire of
        my foes,
    for false witnesses rise up against
        me,
    spouting malicious accusations.

I remain confident of this:
    I will see the goodness of the LORD
        in the land of the living.
Wait for the LORD;
    be strong and take heart
    and wait for the LORD.

Psalm 28

Of David.

To you, LORD, I call;
    you are my Rock,
    do not turn a deaf ear to me.
For if you remain silent,
    I will be like those who go down to
        the pit.
Hear my cry for mercy
    as I call to you for help,
as I lift up my hands
    toward your Most Holy Place.

Do not drag me away with the
        wicked,
    with those who do evil,
who speak cordially with their
        neighbors
    but harbor malice in their hearts.
Repay them for their deeds
    and for their evil work;
repay them for what their hands have
        done
    and bring back on them what they
        deserve.

Because they have no regard for the
        deeds of the LORD
    and what his hands have done,
he will tear them down
    and never build them up again.

Praise be to the LORD,
    for he has heard my cry for mercy.
The LORD is my strength and my
        shield;
    my heart trusts in him, and he helps
        me.
My heart leaps for joy,
    and with my song I praise him.

53

"Let all you do be done in love."

1 Corinthians 16:14

"With God, all things are possible."

Matthew 19:26

GOD'S *Love*

NEVER FAILS

"He makes
all things new."

Revelation 21:5

"THE JOY OF THE LORD
IS YOUR STRENGTH."

Nehemiah 8:10

"Walk by faith, not by sight."

2 Corinthians 5:7

69

BLESSED

HOPEFUL

75

LOVED

77

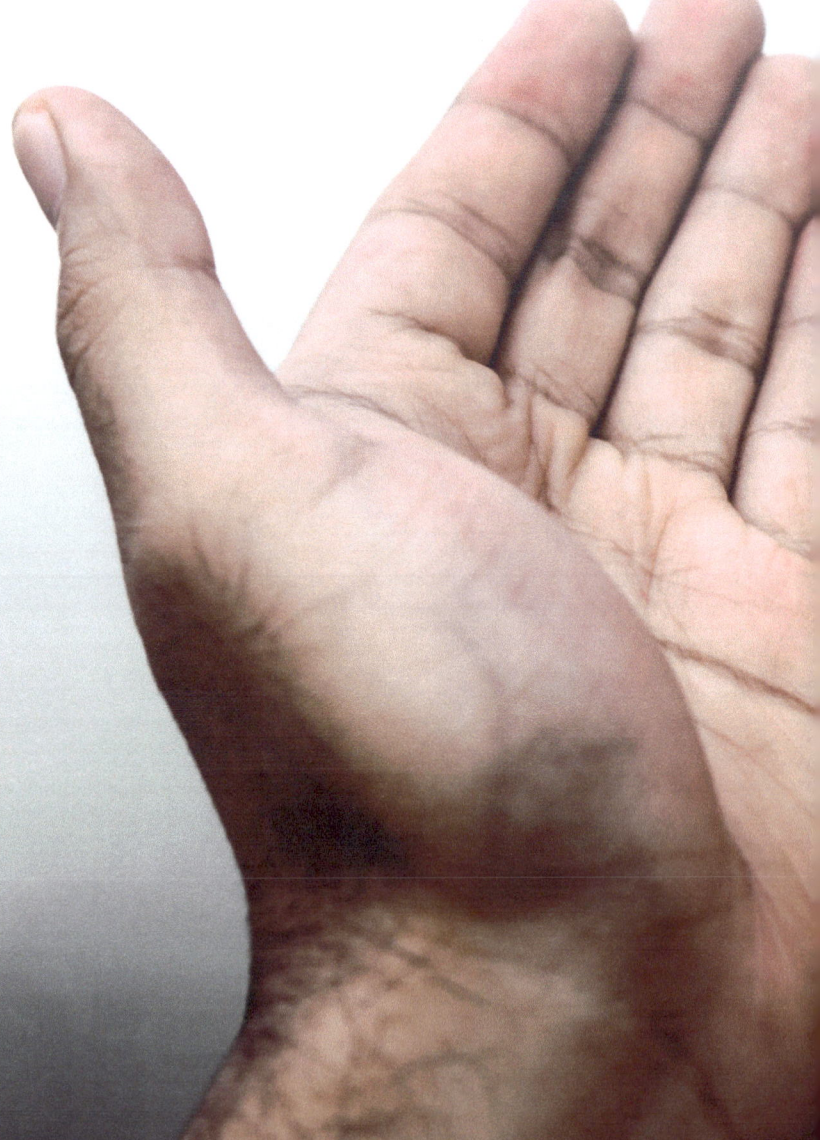

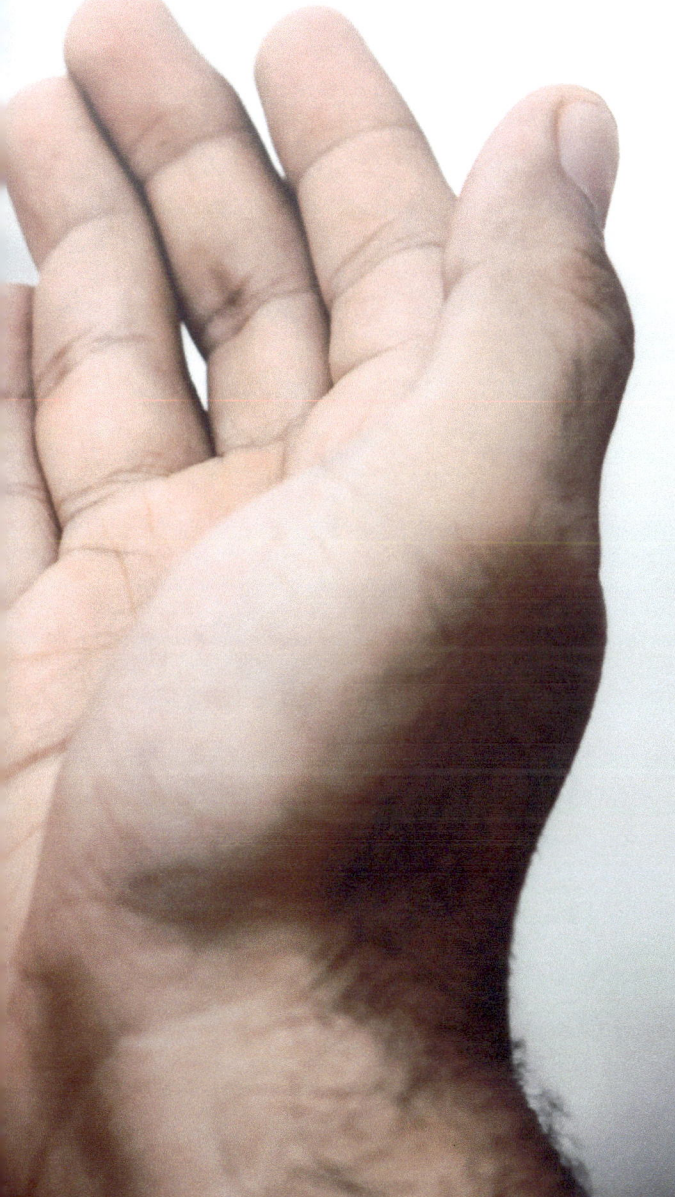

81

"Whatever you ask for in prayer, believe that you have received it, and it will be yours."
Mark 11:24

FAITH

"Your word is a lamp to my feet and a light to my path."

Psalm 119:105

May the God of hope fill you with all joy and peace as you trust in Him, so that you may overflow with hope by the power of the Holy Spirit."

Romans 15:13

Start your day
WITH JESUS

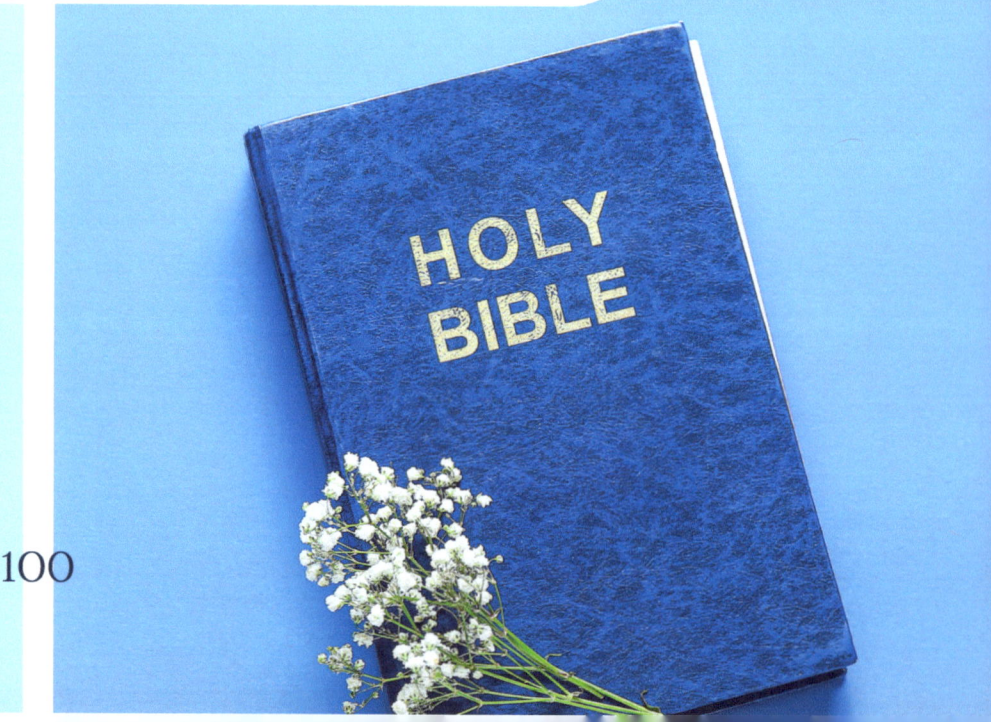

100

GALATIANS 5:22-23

"But the fruit of the Spirit is love, joy, peace, forbearance, kindness, goodness, faithfulness, gentleness and self-control."

PEACE IN HIS PRESENCE

Lord IN YOUR MERCY

108

111

REMINDER
"Even when you can't see it, God is working."

Congregation,
I wish for you...

In the Mighty Name of Jesus,
Amen

www.ingramcontent.com/pod-product-compliance
Lightning Source LLC
Chambersburg PA
CBHW040327090526
44586CB00031B/76